GARDEN ON THE VERGE

GARDEN ON THE VERGE

A NEW APPROACH

GAYLE DALLASTON

SHADY LANES PRESS

COPYRIGHT

First published in Australia in 2025 by Shady Lanes Press

PO Box 1040 Aspley, Queensland 4034, Australia.

CONTENTS

Introduction   vii

PART ONE
WHAT, WHERE, WHY

1. THE PROMISE   3
   We Need More Street Trees   6
   Native Verge Gardens   7
   Turning Ideas into Action   9
   Reduce Risk and Maximise Benefit   10
   Reflection   11

2. WHAT IS A VERGE?   13
   Policy Boundaries   14
   Verges Are Not Community Gardens   14
   Keep It Simple   16
   Reflection   18

PART TWO
HOW DO WE MAKE IT HAPPEN?

3. UNDERSTAND THE SPACE   21
   Gardening In Public   22
   Council Rules   22
   Social Rules   23
   Users and Uses of the Space   24
   Benefits of Working Together   26
   Reflection   27

4. DESIGN FOR PEOPLE & PLANET   29
   Connecting Nature and People   32
   Big Projects or Slow Gardening   32
   Slow Gardening   33
   Start Small - Avoid the Overwhelm   35
   Observe and Experiment   35

Use Plants as Messengers   36
Your Plants in the Wider Environment   37
Your Plants as Advocates   39
Best for People and Planet   40
Reflection   41

5. MANAGE YOUR EXPECTATIONS   43
Good Enough Maintenance   43
Accept Whatever Happens   44
Be Prepared to Lose It All   46
Be Patient and Avoid Conflict   47
Make a Point or Make a Difference   48
Reflection   49

PART THREE
WHAT'S NEXT

6. NURTURE ECOSYSTEMS   53
Framing Our Stories   54
Framing for Focus   55
Reframing as Natural Ecosystems   56
Be Aware of Context   56
Spot and Change the Frames   57
The Civic Ecosystem   58
Reflection   59

CONCLUSION   61
Get Better at Conversations   62
We Learn While Doing   62
Can Verge Gardens Really Change the World?   62

Resources   65
Discussion Questions   66
Simple Cheat Sheet   67
Acknowledgments   69
About the Author   71

INTRODUCTION

Mine was the first verge garden in the street.

When my council introduced a verge garden policy, that was my chance to quit mowing. But where to start?

Buderim Urban Food Streets was being described as a movement for community verge gardening, so we went to have a look. We walked around the streets - on the road because that was the only walkable space. I knew my neighbours would be horrified if I started urban farming in our street. Then the Buderim gardeners had their big dispute with the Sunshine Coast Council.

I didn't want to get into a war with my council, or with my neighbours. No food growing on the verge for me. I just wanted something easier and more rewarding than mowing.

I started a patch at a time, in the smallest, least contentious space. People would stop and talk. What are you doing? Are you allowed to do that? What's that plant?

The shared nature of the space, combined with my activity as the resident-gardener, seemed to give neighbours and strangers permission to stop and ask questions. I met more people in those few months than I had done in the many years we had lived there.

I asked the council for a street tree. Meanwhile, I kept taking out patches of grass and planting as I went. Going slow gave me time to watch how people reacted. It gave time to monitor how I felt about gardening in public too.

When the council put in the little street tree, I planted around the base. As the tree grew, the midgen berry and *Myoporum* plants below captured the falling leaves. The garden was making its own mulch. The tree thrived. It is now the centre-piece of the garden.

My neighbour got a street tree too, but their tree had to cope with grass and the whippersnipper.

The difference in the trees increases every year. While mine thrives, the neighbour's survives.

I began to imagine what the street would be like if it were a long line of thriving street trees supported by native verge gardens. It would add up to a lot of land, and a lot of trees. What if all the streets and suburbs did the same? And all the cities?

I started my verge garden in 2017. Over these years, I have studied what works and what fails, why people give up, why disputes happen, and why some people never start.

This book is to help you avoid the pitfalls and find the easiest, most productive approach to make it happen.

PART ONE
WHAT, WHERE, WHY

1 THE PROMISE

What if we changed the grass in our streets to native gardens?

All that land is there waiting for us to take better care of it. Councils are already planting street trees for shade to cool our cities. Residents already mow the grass.

It's just a small shift in the way we do things.

We go from this…

... to this!

No more mowing! It feels like having a park on your doorstep.

Street trees and native verge gardens are a fast, easy, and low-cost way to create cool, interesting, and healthy streets.

Everyone wins:

- the council's trees thrive,
- the residents have low-maintenance gardens with no mowing,
- and natural biodiversity gets a much-needed boost.

Is it really that easy?

The idea seems simple. So, what is stopping more people shifting from grass to garden?

People are wary for good reason. They often ask:

- Where do you start?
- What about council rules?
- Isn't it just for greenies and activists?
- What if the neighbours object?
- What about disputes?

They sense there is more to this than gardening. This book, combined with your council policy, will help you avoid the pitfalls and give you the confidence to begin.

WE NEED MORE STREET TREES

Tree-lined streets will cool our cities and make walking, cycling, and public transport practical and attractive.

The shade reduces the heat absorbed by hard surfaces, especially roads. That heat, building up during the day and keeping it hot at night, is part of the Urban Heat Island Effect.

When we cool our suburbs, we reduce the impact of extreme heat on our health and the costs of cooling our homes.

Street trees are a long-term proposition. Councils have access to expert knowledge, research, and experience on suitable trees for different environments in a changing climate. They are best at choosing and managing them.

However, just planting trees is not enough. There is not time to wait for saplings to grow into mature trees to cool our streets. This is where verge gardens have a role.

The mixed layers of plants contribute to more complex ecosystems than the two-tier grass and tree landscape common in cities.

The lower-growing plants in the verge gardens help the street trees thrive and form a shady tree canopy faster. Meanwhile, they shade the soil, making our streets cooler and more liveable this year.

NATIVE VERGE GARDENS

Leaving the decisions about street trees to councils still leaves the opportunity for residents to decide what to plant in their verge garden.

Small native shrubs trap fallen leaves to create a natural mulch and build habitat and biodiversity above and below ground level.

Ground cover plants provide a living mulch, hold the soil together, and reduce weeds.

This tree surrounded by a native verge garden thrives.

Perennial and self-seeding plants avoid unnecessary root and soil disturbance for the trees.

The street tree is free from competition from grass and damage from mowing equipment.

We eliminate the noise and emissions of mowing. There are no lawn clippings to wash into stormwater or be dumped in landfill.

Local native gardens also have the same soil requirements as the tree. There is no need to add nutrients that run off to contaminate the stormwater and creek systems. There is no need for herbicides and pesticides when we work with nature.

More rainwater soaks into the ground, replenishing groundwater and reducing downstream flooding.

This tree surrounded by grass and regularly battered by mowing equipment struggles to survive.

Driving and parking on the ground surrounding the trees compacts the soil and damages the roots. Compacted soil sends the roots above the surface for oxygen, only to be scalped by mowers.

TURNING IDEAS INTO ACTION

We must stop expecting someone else to do it all.

Councils and government organisations set policies and plant trees on public land, but they are held back by many residents who refuse to have a street tree in front of their homes.

It needs a new approach where we see ourselves as citizen

gardeners, stewards of the land, contributing to our neighbour-hoods and the wider community.

Residents then work as allies with councils, remembering that everyone who works for a council is also a resident. That means we draw on combined local experience, expertise, and resources.

No extra funding is necessary. Councils already pay for the trees. Residents already mow the grass.

It's the quality of the conversations and the relationships between us that makes change possible.

REDUCE RISK AND MAXIMISE BENEFIT

Council verge garden policies can seem restrictive, but they should be. The policies are designed to reduce the financial and safety risks to gardeners and the wider community.

I recommend going further than many councils by making street trees and native gardens the standard, thereby avoiding the added risks and complications of food growing. Native verge gardens increase the benefits to us all by bringing rich and diverse nature into our everyday lives.

These guiding principles, based on research and experience, will generate the most benefit for you, your street, and city.

1. Comply with your local council policy
2. Respect the needs and views of all potential users and uses of the space
3. Plant predominantly local native plants

These are the key to long-term successful verge gardening for individual residents, and especially for group projects.

When you do this, your native verge garden can be as normal and everyday as grass verges are now.

REFLECTION

The low-key, ordinary feel was the key message in the Gardening Australia story about my verge garden.

It was about the place being comfortable for pedestrians, easy for the postal workers and others going about their work, and the Council's street tree thriving to provide shade for everyone.

You can find the link to the ABC Gardening Australia video on the resources page, or search for "Gardening Australia, Urge to Verge."

---

2 WHAT IS A VERGE?

"The Council are going to destroy our friend's community verge garden," they said. "All that hard work for nothing. We're going to save what we can before the bulldozers move in."

They assumed I would support their cause.

The garden was on the edge of a creek. No sign who was responsible for it. Perhaps their friend lived in one of the many houses or units opposite.

It was a mess. Food plants, herbs, and invasive weeds mixed in with some remnant bushland. Compost bins, old chairs, and jumble lay about.

"He's not been well, so it's got a bit out of hand."

I am not sure what they saw when they looked at it, but I saw an overwhelming job for any gardener to sort out, on a site that would never have gained approval for a genuine community food garden because of the creek and flooding. At most, if they had sufficient volunteers, they might form a bush regeneration group under the guidance of their council.

POLICY BOUNDARIES

To most people, all the public land in parks and around streets and roads is part of a bundle. We have no reason to think about the different types, who owns or is responsible for them, and how that is managed. This can lead to people planting what they think is a verge garden only to find out that they have planted in the wrong place.

The standard verge is the space between your front property line and the kerb, and in line with the fences at the side. Nothing more.

In some Australian states they call it a nature strip. In New Zealand, it is a berm.

Median strips, traffic islands, or laneways are not included. Nor is privately-owned or government-owned land, even if it looks like nobody uses it. If in doubt, check with your council.

The direct link between the verge and the resident is the reason Councils have been able to provide verge garden policies without requirements to go through lengthy processes like formal planning applications or community garden proposals. If there is an issue, they can stand on the verge, look up, and know whose door to knock on.

VERGES ARE NOT COMMUNITY GARDENS

Community gardens have many complications including storage, access to water, community compost, and insurance. You need an incorporated organisation, a constitution, and formal agreements with the relevant council or landowner. Committees handle governance, planning, and management.

Verge garden policies, which allow individual residents to plant in front of their properties, avoid all this.

The complications of verge gardens are different and mainly social, with friction between the competing users and uses of the space. That friction brings challenges and opportunities.

Consider these key differences between community gardens and verge gardens.

Community gardens:

- can be on public or private land with the landowner's agreement.
- are often in parks and private or public space away from footpaths and thoroughfares.
- are restricted to official members and authorised visitors.
- usually concentrate on food growing, composting, training, and group activities.
- involve soil amendments and use of fertilisers, herbicides, and pesticides.
- handle governance with incorporated organisations.
- require committees for administration and organising working bees and rosters.
- are required to have Public Liability Insurance.
- build community as third places where people congregate between work and home.

Verge Gardens:

- are on public land.

- are part of the streets, which are also pedestrian thoroughfares and part of the transport system.
- must be accessible to everyone.
- must fit in with many uses including street trees and wildlife habitat.
- are part of the streetscape and natural ecosystem. Soil amendments and use of fertilisers, herbicides, and pesticides is discouraged.
- have loose governance by council policies and residents.
- place full responsibility for planting and maintenance on the adjacent resident.
- usually have no Public Liability Insurance.
- initiate and build loose community connections as bumping places, where people may have incidental encounters while on their journey.

KEEP IT SIMPLE

To create positive change, you need to understand the space, your own reasons for planting, and why others might not share your passion.

Keeping it simple with local native plants for shade, habitat, and biodiversity is the key to making verge gardens welcomed by the wider community.

Can we do more than just one?

Once we start thinking about verge gardens, we start seeing land everywhere that should be given some love.

But every garden created needs someone to look after it long term. It is better to concentrate on inspiring your neighbours by providing a great example.

We need everyday people converting their own verges and, through that, having conversations designed to inspire their friends and neighbours.

For group projects, your members must all understand and work towards this shared purpose. One member's dispute with neighbours or council could derail your entire project.

Personal Benefits

Understanding and accepting these boundaries helps you get the most benefit for the least effort.

There are mental and physical benefits from connecting with nature, close to home and as part of everyday life.

These gardens are low maintenance and can go weeks or months without care. No mowing in the hot summer sun.

You will learn more about our native plants, nature, and the land you live on.

Goodenia ovata low-growing shrub with small yellow flowers for pollinators.

Social Benefits

Verges as bumping places can play an important part in building connections within a community. Bumping places are where you go from a familiar face, to a nod, to a greeting, to a conversation. You will meet many people you would never otherwise have come across, and some may become friends.

You will grow to understand how all the different organisations interact, and the reasons why many things are not as simple as they first appear.

Residents move from being consumers or critics of government to having more productive civic relationships. These relationships are the foundation for collaborations to create innovative and sustainable solutions.

REFLECTION

Look around your city for verges and nature strips with street trees, verge gardens, both tree and garden, or just grass, and think about how they make you feel.

Are they comforting or hostile? Interesting? Boring? Does the temperature change when you walk in the shade? Do they smell different? Do they change your impression of the house or the neighbourhood?

This is easiest when walking because you are closer and slower, but you can also see verges through the bus window.

Does your impression change if you pass by the same verge regularly?

PART TWO
HOW DO WE MAKE IT HAPPEN?

3 UNDERSTAND THE SPACE

"It would be alright if they were all like that," the councillor said looking at this photo.

This view with a clear path for pedestrians brings people on-side.

GARDENING IN PUBLIC

It was only after I had begun planting on my verge that I realised that it was more than a gardening or landscaping project. It was a social experiment on a very complicated site.

Gardening on the verge is different to gardening inside the fence. It is public land, not yours. Anyone can walk, linger, or gather there.

You can feel very exposed, especially if you are the first in the street. You have no idea how your neighbours will react. Each one will have an opinion on what their street should look like based on their personal values and priorities.

The different viewpoints of neighbours and everyone else who uses the street, combined with formal regulations and unwritten social rules, can turn this shared space that straddles public and private into a battleground.

COUNCIL RULES

Councils see verges as public land used by many different people and services like power, water, and communications. Council staff are familiar with the many uses and users. Official policies and guidelines try to balance competing priorities and risks in a manageable way.

Most importantly, verges are the place for street trees. The cost and responsibility for street trees are borne by councils and their rules reflect that.

Residents taking responsibility for the grass or gardens on the verge keeps the city maintenance costs, and your rates, down.

SOCIAL RULES

Residents view verges in many ways, often depending on context and sometimes contradictory. Pedestrians, cyclists, and motorists, all have their different views about verges even in streets and suburbs far from home.

Social mores and expectations can take you by surprise.

Do you recognise these attitudes?

- If I have to mow it, I should be allowed to do whatever I want.
- It's alright for me and my friends and visitors to park our cars on our verge but not for anyone else.
- I can park my trailer, caravan, or boat on my verge.
- My verge garden is an extension of my own garden.
- Ignore Councils. Ask for forgiveness not permission.
- How dare your dog or child do that on my verge!
- Your messy verge is lowering the tone of the neighbourhood.
- My neatly trimmed lawn is setting a good standard for others to follow.
- That householder is a lawn fanatic and you daren't so much as step on their verge.
- How dare they pick my flowers!
- Anything on the verge is up for grabs.
- Who are those suspicious people walking down our street?

If people feel that you are taking over the public space for your own use, they are likely to get upset. They may push back by damaging your plants.

Be careful not to exclude anyone from this space by blocking paths or making them feel unwelcome, uncomfortable, or unsafe.

When someone is unhappy with your verge garden, they can complain to the Council who must then step in and enforce its policy.

Council rules reduce the physical and legal safety risks. It is up to you to reduce the risk of upsetting your neighbours and wider community.

Councillors and council staff deal with complaints and often get caught up in emotional disputes between residents. No wonder so many are wary of verge gardening.

USERS AND USES OF THE SPACE

I use this exercise for group workshops, but you can also take the challenge yourself.

Consider all the potential users and uses of your verge and share your ideas on a whiteboard. This can lead to lively conversations.

These are common suggestions:

- The resident and their family, friends and visitors
- Neighbours: current and future
- Pedestrians: all ages, all abilities, prams, cyclists, mobility scooters, dog walkers, commuters to bus or train
- Postal and delivery services
- Council workers, including maintenance, street tree planting and care, dealing with complaints
- Meter readers

- Water and power utilities and their workers
- Wheelie bins and kerb-side pickup
- Stormwater to creeks, rainwater infiltration, flood mitigation
- Passengers getting in or out of parked cars
- Motorists on the road or driving in and out of driveways (sightlines)
- People who want to park on the verge
- Street trees for shade
- Nature: biodiversity, habitat, pollinators, wildlife

Your Council has done this for you, thinking about all the things that can go wrong for all these different people and organisations, and for the natural environment, when they design their verge garden guidelines. Behind every restriction is a reason.

Remember to consider pedestrians - all ages and abilities - who might walk along your street, even if they are not locals. How busy is it? Does this vary?

You may know who your current neighbours are, but what about future neighbours? And visitors?

The primary use of the space is for street trees. Street trees are the connections between larger parts of the urban forest. We all need the trees for shade to reduce urban heat. Nature needs them to increase habitat and biodiversity in our cities.

Street trees are essential to reducing urban heat. These readings were taken a few metres apart. The road at 54°C absorbs and stores heat during the day and releases that heat at night to keep our suburbs hotter. The grass on an unshaded verge is better at 38.7°C and the shaded verge garden is just 28.7°C.

Councils work out which trees to plant based on their overall view of the city, knowledge and ongoing research about different species, and historical and social factors. They are also responsible for the cost, maintenance, and liability if a tree causes damage. So, we leave the trees to them.

The approach described in this book minimises everyone's risk of wasting time and resources with disputes. We are allies, creating better streets for people and nature.

Getting to know how the different organisations work and fit within larger systems does more than help us avoid problems. It helps us understand constraints and recognise opportunities.

BENEFITS OF WORKING TOGETHER

Verge gardening is a free and open activity where people can meet.

When we decide we are all on the same side, we build understanding and relationships.

You connect with interesting people with many different skills and backgrounds.

You find local resources, community nurseries, group projects, and examples so you are not alone.

You become part of something much bigger.

It is flexible volunteering without having to commit to go somewhere at set times.

And you gain freedom from mowing that grass!

***

REFLECTION

Find your local council's policy and consider how it aligns with different social attitudes in your neighbourhood.

Try the "Users and Uses" exercise for your verge, preferably as a group.

How do you think your neighbours would react if you planted a verge garden?

Ideas vary within households and between neighbours. Who gets to choose?

***

4 DESIGN FOR PEOPLE & PLANET

Perspectives change when you look at things from different angles.

Is your verge an apron to your house or part of the corridor of the street?

Or viewed from above, are our streets like networks or veins of our cities?

If you only travel by car, you are more likely to see the verge as an apron in front of your home. When you arrive home, it's like a welcome mat, or threshold, or an apron. From inside the property, looking out toward the road, it looks even more like that apron.

Standing in the middle of a verge garden, it can still feel like your territory and part of the street appeal of your house. But turn and look along the street; even better walk along the footpath and approach from different directions.

Orthosiphon aristatus (cat's whiskers) and low-growing ground cover at the side of the pathway

Now you get the pedestrian view of the street, and your verge is one of a long line, and the houses are just bystanders to the main action.

Your verge garden is now part of a corridor. I call it a modern-day "long paddock".

The Australian long paddock was the network of stock routes that threaded around the country, long strips of land between the large paddocks at the side. In times of drought, they were also used to graze stock. The amount of land added up to be much larger than any individual holding.

Our modern-day, urban, long paddock is no stock route. It is the streets reimagined as pollinator corridors, wildlife corridors, and pedestrian pathways threading through our cities.

My verge is no longer a small patch of land in front of my home, but a part of a massive amount of land that forms inter-connecting corridors throughout the suburbs and city.

It is not my land. It is part of the commons, and it connects everybody and everything.

The mulch pathway does more than provide access to the letterbox. It acknowledges the postal workers as part of the community.

CONNECTING NATURE AND PEOPLE

While verge gardens create connections between bigger pieces of habitat, they also help build connections between people and their community, and connections between people and nature.

What you plant, and how you go about it, can make a big difference.

When we slow down, we notice and appreciate nature. This is the trunk of the street tree: *Lophostemon confertus* (Queensland Brush Box)

BIG PROJECTS OR SLOW GARDENING

I have mixed feelings when I see posts on social media showing verge transformation as big landscaping projects with bobcats removing turf and soil and then adding thick mulch.

This might make sense for large projects like microforests and parks but how appropriate is it for suburban verge gardens?

The danger with the big project approach for verge gardeners is, if you change your mind or you get it wrong and your neighbours or council object, there is considerable time and money lost when you have to remove it.

Even when it does work, and it does produce some spectacular gardens, it narrows the focus into what people are doing to nature. There is no room in the big landscaping model for incremental conversations and adapting to feedback from people or working with nature.

SLOW GARDENING

Did I tell you my original motivation was to avoid mowing? I am a lazy gardener without time to spare.

Slow gardening, replacing grass with small tubestock plants until all the grass is gone.

I see the soil life and plant roots as willing helpers that carry on without me between gardening sessions. Or maybe I am their helper.

Most councils, including mine, forbid hard landscaping and garden edges, so it is simply replacing the grass with plants.

Slow gardening means loosening a patch of grass with a fork and removing by hand, replacing it with a little tubestock plant until all the patches meet and there is no grass left.

It means that you:

- avoid damaging underground services or tree roots,
- work with nature to improve the existing soil rather than remove and replace it,
- use plants that need minimal maintenance or watering.

Tubestock and home-propagation is cheap, so you can afford to experiment to find the plants that thrive.

The best time to remove grass and weeds is usually a day or two after the rain when the soil is soft. Get to know your soil and how it reacts. Soil varies, even within one verge.

Stop to ponder and chat to passersby. This is your research. Gardeners using hand tools are much more approachable for questions and conversations than a person with a mower or power tools.

Adjust the design as you get to know the space and see how people move through it.

This is low-risk, incremental gardening to produce biodiverse gardens that will evolve over seasons and years.

Many Council policies encourage this low-key gardening and some state only hand tools are to be used on verge gardens.

START SMALL - AVOID THE OVERWHELM

The concrete path and driveway split my verge garden into four beds. I did the small garden bed closest to the property line first. It was the easiest and least contentious but enough to start conversations with curious neighbours.

I could stop at one patch if I found verge gardening was not for me. Leaving the grass intact until you are ready to plant means you can pause or backtrack. You avoid bare soil turning into a weed bed if you don't work quickly enough.

Slow gardening also gave me time to watch the movements of the postal workers on their bikes and where people walked to cross the road, before I moved on to those sections.

OBSERVE AND EXPERIMENT

Mazus pumilio was a surprise success as a ground cover. It thrived to create a flat green area without mowing.

A major advantage of slow, iterative gardening using cheap

tubestock is mistakes are small. You can build on successes and the lessons you learn along the way.

In practice you, and the weather, and everything else that goes on in your life, will decide how fast or slow you go.

USE PLANTS AS MESSENGERS

As well as signalling some formality to fit the existing character of my street, the *Westringia* shrubs signal the beginning of the verge garden.

Before, and even after, I started this garden, the neighbour's garden maintenance man would stray across the boundary line with his "mow very short and blast the ground with the whipper snipper" routine. To be fair, he probably thought he was doing me a favour. It was time to draw a demarcation line.

Westringia shrubs signal the beginning of the verge garden.

To people who value "flat and neat", anything grass-like looks like it needs mowing. They will mow straight over many plants. While the ground cover beneath the *Westringia* still suffered from being blasted, the shrubs looked sufficiently non-grasslike to escape harm.

Some people will comment on plants they like and ask you where to get them. Increasing everyone's familiarity with our local native plants means they are more likely to choose them for their own gardens.

YOUR PLANTS IN THE WIDER ENVIRONMENT

Verge gardens are a buffer between private properties and the stormwater system so we must avoid mulch and excess nutrients washing into the stormwater.

We also want to avoid spreading weed fragments and seeds by rainwater, wind, or dogs - another reason I prefer native plants and use ground cover plants as living mulch.

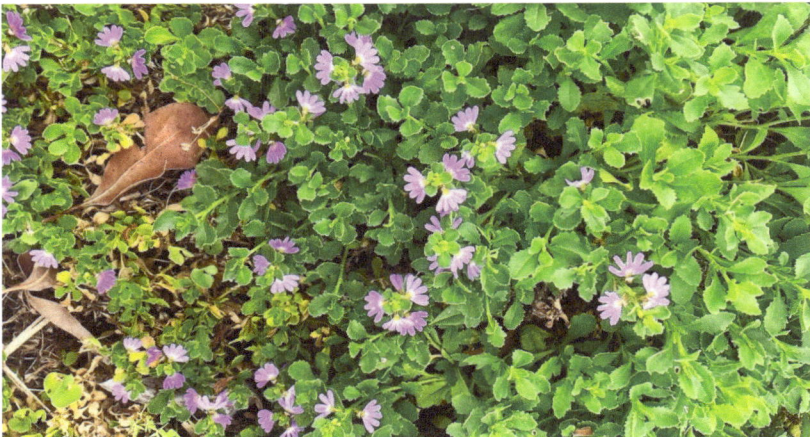

Scaevola, a low-growing native ground cover

Having a creek at the bottom of my hill means I must take extra care about slowing, and not contaminating, stormwater.

If you live near bushland, or shops, a school or a pub, that may also affect your choices.

Most councils have a list of recommended plants. Canberra has two lists; one is for fire prone areas.

Look at what grows well inside your garden or in your suburb and ask for advice from your local community nursery. If you have a Gardens for Wildlife or similar scheme in your area, they can also help with local knowledge. When searching online, always check the location. Suitable plants in one region may be weeds in another.

Even then, you might find some plants do better than you expect while some fail to thrive. My garden is now old enough that I have replaced many plants.

Dianella is an attractive plant for verges with dainty flowers for the bees and purple berries for birds. Unfortunately, young plants often get mistaken for grass. The leaves are softer than *Lomandra*. With all plants, ensure they are far enough from the path to avoid being trip hazards.

If some parts of your council's policy seem frustrating or irrelevant to you, accept them anyway. As you learn more about the issues, the restrictions make more sense.

You still have plenty of scope for creativity and personal preferences within their guidelines.

With multiple native verge gardens in a street, each planted with that individual gardener's preferences, we will get plenty of biodiversity.

YOUR PLANTS AS ADVOCATES

People like flowers. As well as providing for our pollinators, flowers help your neighbours accept and appreciate your verge garden.

Hibbertia scandens can be grown as a climber or scrambler. The bright yellow flowers attract several varieties of native bee.

Flowers add interest and provide conversation starters with the changing seasons.

Annuals fill gaps while your tubestock shrubs grow. Some self-seed for ongoing displays.

Many attractive native plants are not well known or available from major commercial nurseries. Including these on your verge will provide habitat for our native bees and butterflies, and make the plants better known in the community.

BEST FOR PEOPLE AND PLANET

By considering how to get the best social and environmental outcomes with the resources at hand, you create much more doable and rewarding projects.

Using local native plants suited to your climate and soil means they are more likely to grow well without needing water or soil amendments.

Once the garden is established, it is low maintenance and much less work than grass. Your garden can go for long periods where you do no more than pull out the odd weed.

You will have created a community asset and personal connections in your neighbourhood.

Watch and listen for interactions between the plants and the people walking and cycling. I have been surprised by:

- the elderly lady reaching out and touching flowers
- a teenager pausing to pick a paper daisy as she walked by with her friends
- grandparents talking to children: "I haven't seen one of those flowers since I was a little girl"

- neighbourhood children collecting flowers for a school project

---

REFLECTION

My single verge garden has created 58 square meters of biodiverse habitat with more than 20 species of local native plants, within the existing council policy.

If 2 out of 3 of the residents in my council ward planted out just 40 square metres it would create 50 hectares of biodiverse habitat supporting street trees and creating green, shady, nature corridors.

If 2 out of 3 of the residents in the Brisbane City Council area planted, it would create 1000+ hectares of biodiverse habitat and transform the city - without the need to buy any land.

Can you do some calculations for your street, suburb, or city?

What other benefits might a verge transformation bring? Whose lives would it change? What would it make possible?

---

5 MANAGE YOUR EXPECTATIONS

Even though you look after it, you do not own the verge. You have no more rights over that land than anyone else. You have no control over who uses the space.

People might not notice, or admire, or even respect your garden.

The more money or emotion you invest in the garden, the more it will hurt if your plants are trampled, broken, or stolen.

GOOD ENOUGH MAINTENANCE

When my verge garden is looking a bit drab or some weeds have come up, I remind myself that it still looks better, and functions better, than a grass verge.

A good-enough verge garden is more likely to be accepted because it looks like someone cares for it but does not fuss over it. Remember, people need to be able to walk down the street without feeling like they are intruding in someone's treasured, private garden.

As with housework, there are tricks where one small thing can change what people notice.

For example, an occasional straight edge can make the whole garden look neater.

Create straight edges on the borders between grass and garden with a spade. Garden edging is not allowed as it can be a trip hazard.

Think back to the earlier steps where you reflected on your reactions to other people's gardens. Where is that "good enough" line for you?

ACCEPT WHATEVER HAPPENS

This is public land, so you will have dogs marking their territory, and people walking on your plants, picking off pieces or even taking whole plants.

Using tubestock and cuttings, especially in vulnerable spots, will reduce your losses. I also see gardening as growing biodiversity within the soil, so plants that come and go fit into my plan.

Tubestock from local community nurseries. Return or reuse the tubes (square pots) for propagation.

Apart from the Council's street tree, the only expensive plant was a gift specifically for the verge. It is a little low-growing banksia, perfectly shaped with three branches. I planted it close to the tree. The next morning, one of those three branches was snapped off. The not-so-perfect banksia is still there.

I have had the wheelie bins dragged across the garden, tradespeople stomping through the middle, people picking flowers, and of course there are the dogs.

Myoporum boninense ssp.australe (Boobialla) is so hardy they put it on median strips. It provides food and habitat for wildlife

Helpful neighbours and their paid gardeners will mow any prized plants that look remotely like grass.

It pays to keep your special plants, along with features like pots and birdbaths, inside the fence.

BE PREPARED TO LOSE IT ALL

The verge can be dug up, often without notice for services like power and water.

The space available can change as our cities grow and change, and housing or infrastructure is added.

When there is a complaint, anything that is outside the guide-lines must go.

When there is a change or a dispute, the angry response from residents often stems from being unprepared for this loss.

So, how do you cope?

One way is to see what has happened as a learning experience.

Remind yourself that the soil health has improved so the next plants will have a head start.

Remember all the conversations and the experiences you and your garden have already created. They are not lost.

Then you keep the garden evolving, making sure you stay within the latest guidelines, and incorporating all the lessons you have learned.

BE PATIENT AND AVOID CONFLICT

Planting a vegetable patch or a wild garden would have upset some neighbours in my very "hedge and lawn" street even though it would have been within Council guidelines.

Slow change, being willing to talk about what you are doing in a thoughtful and respectful way and not veering too far from the current social norms reassures neighbours that you are intent on improving the street, not disrupting it. You may find a lot more allies than you expect.

Over the years, as neighbours have adapted, my garden has grown a little less formal. However, the emphasis on being low-key and comfortable for pedestrians is as strong as ever.

MAKE A POINT OR MAKE A DIFFERENCE

Some verge gardeners describe what they are doing as a protest or as guerrilla gardening. They resent council rules and see no reason why they should follow them.

I cover this more in group and collaboration projects but for individual gardeners, here are a few thoughts:

- You can be confrontational, dig your heels in and fight, or you can just get on with making a difference - improving your street, inspiring neighbours, and learning more about nature and this complicated space.
- In the same way that I wanted to stop wasting time and resources mowing to maintain an unchanging grass verge, I try to avoid wasting time, energy, or resources on skirmishes.
- I like to play the long game. My focus is on achieving mainstream action to increase biodiversity, to green and cool our cities, and for everyone to collaborate on doing as much as we can, as fast as we can, for a liveable city and sustainable future.
- We get there by concentrating on what is doable, creating a series of small incremental wins, localising and adapting where necessary.

Participants in group projects need regular, ongoing conversations to ensure individual motivations and expectations are aligned with the group's overall purpose.

REFLECTION

What is your motivation and what outcomes do you want from your verge garden?

How do you think you will cope with setbacks?

Would being part of a group project help get you started and keep you motivated?

PART THREE
WHAT'S NEXT

6 NURTURE ECOSYSTEMS

In June 2025, the ABC published two stories about the failure of my local Council to meet targets for tree canopy and tree health.

On social media, commenters blamed the Council, development, increased housing density, and political rivals. Many held today's experts responsible for decisions made generations ago.

The difficulty increasing tree canopy is occurring around the country with all councils, not just mine.

It is easy to say councils should plant more trees and look after them better. From the work I have done, I know it is not that simple. For a start, a surprising number of residents refuse to accept a street tree in front of their homes and they will destroy any tree planted there.

FRAMING OUR STORIES

The stories we tell and share, whether they are professional journalism or everyday anecdotes, frame the way we think.

Linear stories are easy.

1. We need more street trees.
2. It is council's job to make it happen.
3. They have failed to meet targets.
4. Council has failed.

There is no role in that story for anyone who damages trees, apart from a fleeting reference that Energex removes or prunes trees for safety.

There is no room for the many residents who refuse to have a street tree.

There is no discussion of the space made unavailable for planting by giving priority to roads, free on-street parking, and wide intersections.

And there is no room in the story for native verge gardens like mine to protect and help street trees thrive. Verge gardens are a different topic and have their own stories.

Most verge garden stories are just as limiting.

Some urban food growers want to claim the space for growing food to share. Street trees are not included in these stories apart from warnings that councils will object if you damage their trees. Pedestrians are not part of the story either; they can walk on the road and are portrayed as a nuisance if they complain about the garden impeding or blocking their path.

Pollinator corridor advocates often leave out the need for accessible paths and street trees.

We have many linear and narrow stories that limit our view of complex problems and thereby limit the ways we might address the complex and interlinked challenges of sustainability.

At best, these stories and conversations keep us stuck where we are. More often, they take us in the wrong direction. The divisions between the residents and councils increase. More moderate residents become cautious of verge gardening. Opportunities to make our cities more resilient in a changing climate never get the chance to emerge.

FRAMING FOR FOCUS

We need to zoom in with narrow frames to define and focus on solvable problems with solutions based on data, logic, and specialist technical knowledge.

When we zoom in on the more complex problem of greening the streets:

- We talk about street trees as a standalone topic and decide which species to plant where.
- We talk about verge gardens as a different topic and formulate guidelines and policies.
- We can even talk about each plant individually to choose plants for each location.

When someone tells a story, they get to choose the frame. The easiest thing to do is accept and follow their frame without question. Angry Facebook comments on the tree canopy story are just following the cues.

If you are on the receiving end of the blame in these stories, you might try to refute or deny it, make excuses, or shift the blame. That leads to more finger-pointing but no solutions.

REFRAMING AS NATURAL ECOSYSTEMS

For complex, interlinking problems where technical solutions are not enough, we need to be able to zoom out to allow for more diverse perspectives, knowledge, and expertise to contribute and combine. This wider discussion enables cross-discipline and cross-sector collaborations.

I choose to tell the verge garden story within a wider frame of residents and councils working together to nurture social and natural ecosystems. Green streets are where the urban forest coexists with the social and transport systems of a liveable city.

The photos of corridor view of a shaded pathway reinforce that message. It provides the wider shared purpose from which you can zoom in to see individual garden beds and plants.

In practice, we need to be able to move smoothly between them, connecting and combining the big picture and the close focus where we all have our individual interests and expertise.

BE AWARE OF CONTEXT

We all have words we use within our disciplines where we can be reasonably sure the meaning is shared. To outsiders, it can sound like jargon.

It can be confusing when words are used in a scientific sense and as part of general discourse.

For example, biodiversity will mean something vastly different to an ecologist, a landscape architect, and a casual gardener.

In complex discussions, everybody needs to be alert that they might have a mismatch of understanding, not just expert to non-expert, but between disciplines.

Listen carefully, be quick to clarify, and slow to judge.

SPOT AND CHANGE THE FRAMES

What happens when we widen the frame and talk about what grows in our streets as natural ecosystems with constant and evolving interaction, co-dependency, and mutually beneficial relationships?

The street tree benefits from the surrounding native verge garden. The verge garden benefits from the shade and shelter of the tree. Wildlife benefits from more diverse habitat. Any change to one part of this ecosystem will affect other parts.

We can frame a single street tree and the verge garden around it as interrelated within one verge, and then widen the frame to see them as part of connecting ecosystem and stories with the whole street, the stormwater and the creeks.

Our wider frame excludes activities like growing food or exotic invasive plants on the verge. It can allow for community food growing whereby the food grown inside the fence benefits from the increased pollinator activity and excess produce is shared in a box at the gate.

In our stories, the practice of verge gardening is complementary to the expertise and knowledge of the many professions that feed into the management of public land and design of our streets. Using this wider ecosystem frame increases diversity of participants and the resources at hand to improve the sustainability of our cities.

By working together, we achieve more than any of us could do alone. We are allies, all on the same side.

THE CIVIC ECOSYSTEM

The natural ecosystem approach is reflected in the people involved.

We start to develop another type of ecosystem – the networks of people who have built mutually beneficial relationships and trust through the localised activity of verge gardening and tree planting.

- We stop wasting energy fighting and competing.
- We gain hope and energy from sharing ideas and small shared wins.
- We share and leverage our successes.

This is how we scale, not top-down or bottom-up but replicable, localised, collaborative projects.

We nurture natural ecosystems of trees and a native understory, threading through our cities connecting larger areas of green space to help make our cities cooler and more resilient.

In the process, we create the opportunity to nurture civic ecosystems of councils, community organisations, research organisations, businesses, and individuals all sharing and working towards a future where nature and people thrive.

We connect with each other through language, stories, and conversations.

When we follow this path…

- We stop falling for false promises with simple solutions.
- We stop feeling helpless and stuck.
- We embrace the interlinked nature of the issues we face.
- We see opportunity and hope in acknowledged complexity.
- We address multiple issues with every action.
- We find more resources and energy in collaborations.
- We scale outwards (like natural ecosystems.)

REFLECTION

This is a broad and far-reaching topic that feeds into group projects, networks, and collaborations. Even if you are hesitant to go that far, some awareness will help you make sense of what is happening in our complex world.

For the many professionals and advocates who know some of the technical solutions for sustainability but can't get them implemented, civic networks are a key part of forming the cross-discipline and cross-sector collaborations needed.

Which sectors do you struggle with? Whose support would make the difference you need?

CONCLUSION

When I started this journey in 2017, I felt there was nothing I could do about the big issues we face with changing climate and the need to transition to a more sustainable world. That was for governments to work out and they were not doing a good job of it. It all came down to what people would vote for.

I had retreated into my local world, recycling, organic gardening, doing what I could.

The experience of verge gardening, and the resulting conversations opened another world for me.

Conversations are the key. The way we talk about what we do shapes our understanding of the world and what is possible. The way we talk to each other determines the levels of trust and motivation that emerges.

We move in the direction of our conversations.

GET BETTER AT CONVERSATIONS

We need more practice at slow, thoughtful conversations in our busy world. Media stories are fast and simple, social media amplifies the simplistic blame games, advertising promises us easy answers to all our problems.

Rather than accept or repeat their stories or frames, we can replace them with our own.

WE LEARN WHILE DOING

The only way to learn this is by reflective practice. You start with the doable, always experimenting, reflecting, adapting, refining.

Your verge offers the perfect stage for starting and practicing conversations. The most productive conversations come within the frame of citizens planting verge gardens to support council street trees.

If you do this, you will have done your bit to improve your neighbourhood and city.

If you want to do more, and I hope you do, you can use the experience on your verge to develop your skills and then join a group or community project, or start your own. We explore that in the Shady Lanes Substack community and the second book in this series. From there you can move on to more complex collaborations.

CAN VERGE GARDENS REALLY CHANGE THE WORLD?

For me, verge gardens and streets connect everything. Bringing all the competing users and uses, different disciplines, and different sectors, crashing together in our hyperlocal commons creates a unique opportunity.

That is where we can learn how to manage the conversations to nurture innovative collaborations to tackle complex problems.

We grow natural ecosystems on the verge and develop people ecosystems around it. We scale outwards with localised, adaptive, replication just like nature does.

By working together, we can make the promise of verge gardens come true.

RESOURCES

See The Shady Lanes Project for:

- a directory of policies. Every council is different. Find or add your local policy.
- Three Guiding Principles.
- Understanding the Space articles.
- book sales and services.
- ABC Gardening Australia, Urge to Verge, media, and awards.

shadylanes.com.au

Join the Shady Lanes Substack as a free or paid subscriber for:

- regular newsletters,
- articles and resources for your group,
- discussions, Q&A, support to run your group projects.

DISCUSSION QUESTIONS

For book clubs and group workshops:

- What ideas in this book resonated with you?
- Has this changed the way you see your street? If so, how?
- Did any users or uses of the street surprise you?
- How important do you think the relationship is between councils and residents?
- Would you convert your own verge? Why or why not?
- Would you consider joining or starting a group project?
- How might this local action relate to issues like sustainable transport, urban design, and active lifestyles?
- How might this local action relate to global action on climate change?

SIMPLE CHEAT SHEET

1. Read your local council's policy.
2. Know the boundaries.
3. Get to know the space from many angles.
4. Where do you need to leave space clear for pedestrians, passengers from parked cars, postal and delivery workers, and meter readers?
5. If you have a street tree, take care not to disturb or damage the roots.
6. What is the easiest and least contentious space?
7. Choose your plants.
8. Plant local native plants from community nurseries.
9. Consider flowers that delight people.
10. Do it bit by bit. Stand back and watch how it changes the space. Watch how people react. Reflect on how you react.

See a longer version and join the discussion in "Understanding the Space" on the Shady Lanes Substack

shadylanesproject.substack.com

ACKNOWLEDGMENTS

A verge garden is a collaborative and evolving venture and so was this book.

I thank the Brisbane City Council officers for their patience and professionalism in answering my questions over the years.

For the insights into diverse collaborations with loose networks, thank you to Ed Morrison for his research that underpins Strategic Doing. For assistance in shaping this book and helping me realise that I am to write three books, not one, thank you to Kelly Irving and the Expert Author Community.

To my local ACF Community Brisbane Northside group and the Banyo verge gardeners and community, thank you for your ongoing willingness to engage and experiment.

Thank you also to the readers and subscribers of the Shady Lanes Substack for your support.

On a personal note, I must thank my husband, Ken, for his ongoing support of the Shady Lanes Project, and for photography and book design.

And finally, to you the reader: thank you for taking the potential of verge gardening seriously. We are all on the same side.

ABOUT THE AUTHOR

Gayle Dallaston works across disciplines, connecting people with diverse ideas and perspectives to create innovative solutions to complex problems.

She writes extensively on how everyday conversations and stories are the key to creating a strong civic society where people and nature thrive.

In 2025, Gayle received a TREENET Gold Leaf Award in Community Urban Forestry for her work on The Shady Lanes Project.

She lives in Brisbane and shares a garden with varied wildlife including birds, blue tongue lizards, and a ring-tailed possum.

You can connect with Gayle in the following ways:

- Website: www.gayledallaston.com
- Substack: substack.com/@gayledallaston
- LinkedIn: www.linkedin.com/in/gayledallaston

www.ingramcontent.com/pod-product-compliance
Lightning Source LLC
Chambersburg PA
CBHW041308020426
42333CB00001B/10